TALES OF THE DEAD

ANCIENT ROME

Written by Stewart Ross
Consultant Dr Hugh Bowden
Illustrated by Inklink & Richard Bonson

DK

LONDON, NEW YORK, MUNICH,
MELBOURNE AND DELHI

EDITOR Kate Simkins
ART EDITOR/STORY VISUALISER John Kelly
ART DIRECTOR Mark Richards
PUBLISHING MANAGER Simon Beecroft
PUBLISHER Alex Allan
PRODUCTION Erica Rosen
DTP DESIGNER Lauren Egan

First published in Great Britain in 2005 by
Dorling Kindersley Limited, 80 Strand, London WC2R 0RL
A Penguin Company

04 05 10 9 8 7 6 5 4 3 2 1

Colour reproduction by Colourscan, Singapore
Printed and bound by Leo Paper Products, China

Discover more at
www.dk.com

ACKNOWLEDGMENTS

Richard Bonson painted the fort (pages 6–7), villa (pages 16–17), street scene (pages 20–21)
and Colosseum (pages 28–29).

Inklink painted all other artworks, including the graphic novel.

CONTENTS

BUILT FOR BLOOD

Finished in 80 CE, the Colosseum was a gigantic open-air stadium in which entertainments took place for the citizens of Rome. It seated 50,000 excited spectators. The shows were often bloodthirsty and included gladiator fights to the death.

ROMAN POWER

The ancient Romans created one of the richest and best-organised civilisations the world has ever seen. The Roman civilisation dominated Europe, the Middle East and North Africa. Its law, language and culture have had a lasting influence on the modern world. Roman power was based on a vast empire of lands conquered and maintained by the mighty Roman army. Under the army's protection, citizens of Rome enjoyed peace and prosperity. But the Empire thrived on slavery, and anyone who dared to resist the command of Rome was crushed by the army without mercy.

MEET THE CHARACTERS...

PUBLIUS
"OK, so maybe I don't get on with Sabina that well. But since our mum died, my sister's been so bossy – and she reckons she's a better rider than me. I want to be a Roman soldier like my dad when I grow up. We're really proud – they've just made him a Roman citizen!"

SABINA
"I'm only a year older than my ten-year-old brother Publius, but I'm so much more grown up than him. He's a typical boy who thinks he can do everything really well. Actually, I can ride better than he can, and I understand things that he doesn't, like what Roman citizenship really means to us."

JUBA
"Life has not been easy since my wife died last year, especially with my work as an auxiliary soldier and two children to keep an eye on. The future's bright, though, because my military service has given me the greatest reward of all – Roman citizenship. At last I feel like a real person."

TIMELINE

1969
American astronauts land on the Moon

1492
Columbus sails to America

1275
Genghis Khan conquers Asia

410 CE
City of Rome invaded by barbarians

27 BCE
Augustus becomes first Roman emperor

509
Rome expels its king and becomes a republic

4

PRESENT DAY

2000 CE (COMMON ERA)   1000 CE   CE BCE

STORY CONTINUES ON NEXT PAGE

THE TERROR TRAIL

North Africa, 145 CE. Local tribes have been making trouble for Roman troops, and the Emperor Antoninus Pius is determined to put a stop to the rebellion. As you read on, explore the contrasting lives of the citizens and slaves, and rich and poor, who lived in one of the world's most powerful civilisations.

THE ROMAN FORT AT SITIFIS, MAURETANIA.

YOU HAVE SERVED ROME WELL, JUBA.

YOUR ROMAN CITIZENSHIP IS WELL DESERVED.

THANK YOU, COMMANDER HORTALUS.

HORTALUS
"I've quite liked my time in Mauretania, although things have been a bit tricky recently. The locals are mostly OK, and I've made some good friends, like Juba. Anyway, I'm handing over command of my legion and heading back to Rome to serve as a senator. I must say, I'm looking forward to it."

BRUTUS
"My business is slaves. People always need slaves and I've got good contacts. I can generally find what my customers want — young, mature, male, female. No point in being sentimental about it."

THE ROMAN WORLD

The Roman Empire was named after its capital city, Rome, in central Italy. The city was surrounded by fertile farmland, and it became rich and powerful. Rome built up a huge army and began conquering other lands. These lands became part of the Roman Empire, ruled by the Emperor in Rome. The Empire was at its most powerful in the second century CE.

NORTH AMERICA   EUROPE   ASIA
SOUTH AMERICA   AFRICA

ITALY
Rome
GREECE
Sitifis
Carthage
MAURETANIA
AFRICA
Mediterranean Sea

753
Traditional date for the founding of the city of Rome

c.1400
Civilisation emerges on mainland Greece

c.2000
Minoan civilisation develops on the island of Crete

c.2500
Indus Valley civilisation flourishes in Pakistan

c.3100
King Menes unites Egypt

1000 BCE (BEFORE COMMON ERA)   2000 BCE   3000 BCE

CONTINUED FROM PREVIOUS PAGE →

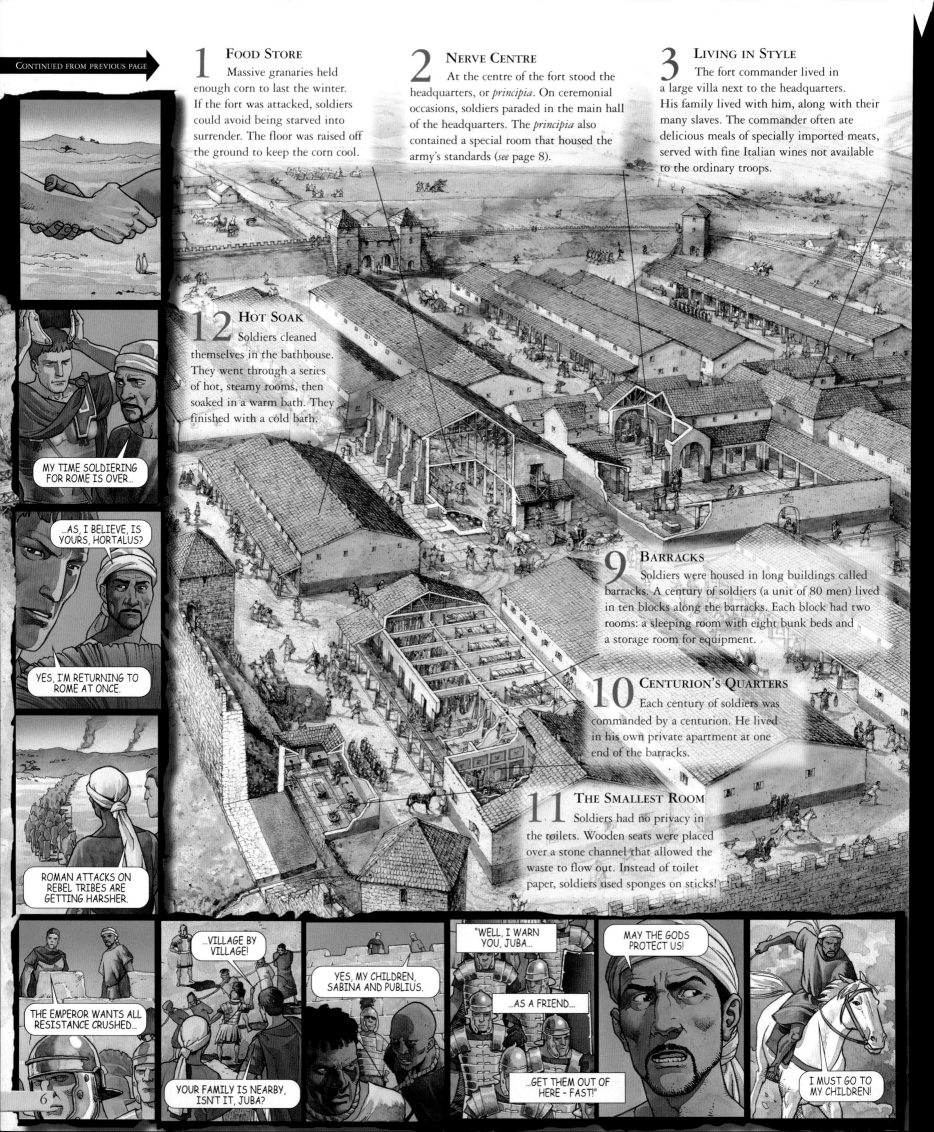

1 FOOD STORE
Massive granaries held enough corn to last the winter. If the fort was attacked, soldiers could avoid being starved into surrender. The floor was raised off the ground to keep the corn cool.

2 NERVE CENTRE
At the centre of the fort stood the headquarters, or *principia*. On ceremonial occasions, soldiers paraded in the main hall of the headquarters. The *principia* also contained a special room that housed the army's standards (*see page 8*).

3 LIVING IN STYLE
The fort commander lived in a large villa next to the headquarters. His family lived with him, along with their many slaves. The commander often ate delicious meals of specially imported meats, served with fine Italian wines not available to the ordinary troops.

12 HOT SOAK
Soldiers cleaned themselves in the bathhouse. They went through a series of hot, steamy rooms, then soaked in a warm bath. They finished with a cold bath.

9 BARRACKS
Soldiers were housed in long buildings called barracks. A century of soldiers (a unit of 80 men) lived in ten blocks along the barracks. Each block had two rooms: a sleeping room with eight bunk beds and a storage room for equipment.

10 CENTURION'S QUARTERS
Each century of soldiers was commanded by a centurion. He lived in his own private apartment at one end of the barracks.

11 THE SMALLEST ROOM
Soldiers had no privacy in the toilets. Wooden seats were placed over a stone channel that allowed the waste to flow out. Instead of toilet paper, soldiers used sponges on sticks!

4 A Soldier's Duties
Soldiers didn't just fight. They also went on guard duty, policed the nearby towns, tended to the fort's horses, and washed clothes and bedding. One of the worst jobs must have been cleaning the toilets, which often became blocked!

FRONTIER FORT

STORY CONTINUES ON NEXT PAGE ➡

The Romans built huge, fortified camps along their frontiers. The job of the soldiers who lived in the forts was to keep invaders out and uphold law and order among local populations. Forts were made of stone, brick, wood and earth. They were like small towns. Some covered up to 22 hectares (54 acres), larger than 44 football pitches! Inside, the soldiers had everything they needed – housing, food supplies, workshops, stables, offices, baths and a medical centre.

"ROME WILL PROTECT US!"

5 Going to Town
Towns grew up around the forts. Here, traders encouraged soldiers to spend their pay on goods and services, including food and wine. Some soldiers secretly married local women.

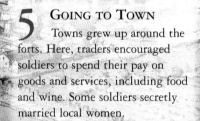

LISTEN, CHILDREN! I'VE BEEN MADE A ROMAN CITIZEN.

7 Tending to the Sick
Wounded soldiers were cared for in the hospital. Doctors cleaned and bandaged wounds. With so many soldiers living in cramped quarters, disease was common.

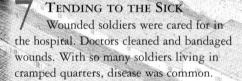

"WE'VE VERY LITTLE TIME!"

6 Gate Defences
After a patrol's regular tour of the surrounding area, it marches through the fort's main gate. Most forts had four gates, each defended by heavily guarded towers.

8 Walled In
The stone walls were up to 2 metres (6½ feet) thick and reinforced with a bank of earth. They were surrounded by a deep ditch and were extremely difficult to knock down.

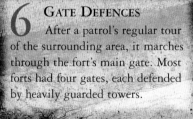

...TO DESTROY THE VILLAGE!

LET ME THROUGH! EMERGENCY!

RACE YOU TO HIM!

IT'S FATHER!

NOT A HOPE, SLOWCOACH!

THE ROMANS ARE COMING...

MILITARY MACHINE

The Roman army was one of the finest fighting forces ever created. The Romans owed everything to it. Their army was the force that created the Empire and kept it together. Emperors were expected to be soldiers, and a successful soldier sometimes became emperor.

KEEPING UP STANDARDS

The most prized possession of an army legion was its standard, a kind of banner with an eagle that symbolised Rome. Soldiers would rather die than surrender it. Smaller units called centuries had their own standards.

Cavalryman

Archer

Slinger

Centurion

Standard bearer

Legionary soldier

Javelin (*pilum*) for throwing and stabbing

Padded iron helmet protecting the face as well as the head

Flexible plate armour tied together with wire

Soldier's carrying crossbar hung with three days' rations, water, a blanket and other useful items

Auxiliary soldier – a non-Roman (like Juba) who fought for Rome

Short stabbing sword in scabbard

Leather sandals studded with iron

Leather-covered plywood shield

THE BACKBONE OF THE ARMY

The Roman army was professional. This meant its troops were paid for being soldiers. Legionary foot soldiers were the main force of the army. These highly trained citizens served for 25 or 26 years. They had to be fit and strong and able to swim and ride as well as fight. If they were not killed, they retired as wealthy and respected men.

REMEMBER, CHILDREN...

...WHATEVER HAPPENS - YOUR FATHER IS A ROMAN CITIZEN!

WAIT HERE! I'LL TALK TO THEIR COMMANDER.

FATHER RODE BRAVELY TOWARDS THE ROMANS...

THEY'LL LISTEN TO A FELLOW ROMAN.

IN THE NAME OF...

TAKE AIM...

SHOOT!

URGHHH!

THEY'VE SHOT JUBA! WE'RE UNDER ATTACK!

FATHER!

Legion of
10 cohorts

STORY CONTINUES ON NEXT PAGE

THE LEGION

The Roman army was made up of legions, each containing about 5,500 male citizens. In Juba's time, about 30 legions were based throughout the Empire, expanding its frontiers and putting down revolts. Each legion was known by a number and was intensely proud of its record and traditions.
Its commander was a *legatus*, who took his orders directly from the Emperor.

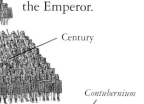

Cohort

COHORT: 480 men
A legion was divided into 10 cohorts. The first cohort of 800 men was the most important. The other 9 cohorts had 480 men each.

CENTURY: 80 men
A century, commanded by an experienced and battle-hardened centurion, was the legion's key fighting unit. The first cohort had 10 centuries. The others had 6 centuries.

CONTUBERNIUM: 8 men
The smallest army group was the *contubernium*, meaning 'tent-full'. Its soldiers shared a tent and a mule while on the march and two rooms when in camp.

Century

Contubernium

Legionary soldier

LAYING SIEGE

The Romans were experts at siege warfare. When a fortified town refused to surrender, the soldiers built ramps against the walls, bombarded the walls with stones and hammered at the gates with massive battering rams. Soldiers climbed over the walls on siege towers. No mercy was shown when a rebel town fell – it was often burned to the ground and all the inhabitants killed.

A commander heads a triumphant procession through the streets of Rome.

TRIUMPH!

When a commander had killed over 5,000 enemies in a campaign, he was given a 'triumph'. This was a spectacular ceremony in Rome. Soldiers and city officials headed a procession that included prisoners of war and loot and passed through specially built triumphal arches. By Juba's time, only the emperors celebrated triumphs, even though other men had done the fighting!

Siege tower covered with dampened hides to prevent it being set on fire

Machine for firing enormous bolts (arrows)

Unarmoured locals working for the Romans

Giant bow

Loading a stone into a siege catapult

Legionary soldiers ready to climb into the siege tower

WHAT HAVE WE HERE?

SUDDENLY...

THEN, THERE WAS SILENCE.

THE SOUNDS OF BATTLE WENT ON AND ON.

DIE, BARBARIANS!

THWAAACK!

GET INSIDE!

WE CLUNG TOGETHER, TERRIFIED BY WHAT WE HAD SEEN...

...WHILE OUTSIDE...

...THE VILLAGERS FOUGHT FOR THEIR LIVES...

...AGAINST THE INVINCIBLE ROMANS.

MANY PEOPLES, ONE EMPIRE

The greatest Roman achievement was creating an empire from many different cultures. They managed this by making membership of the Empire desirable – people were generally safer and better off under Roman rule than outside it. Territories under Roman rule were called provinces.

GERMANS
Only a few of the tribes of Germani (Germans) were absorbed into the Roman Empire. Their frontier with Rome was often at the centre of fierce fighting.

BRITONS
The Romans conquered southern Britain (Britannia) in the first century CE. They built Hadrian's Wall to keep out the Scots.

DACIANS
Dacia (modern Romania) was conquered by Emperor Trajan in 106 CE. The victory was commemorated in carvings on Trajan's column in Rome.

GAULS
The Gauls lived in what is now France, Belgium, Switzerland, Austria and northern Italy. These Celtic lands were taken into the Roman Empire over many years.

ROMANS
The tribes of central Italy were the first Romans. As they conquered lands and people, they spread their way of life over a vast area.

SPANIARDS
Spain, then called Hispania, became part of the Roman Empire over many years. Many senators, writers and orators came from Spain, as did the Emperor Trajan.

Rome ●

MAURETANIANS
Sabina and Publius were from Mauretania. Although many local people resisted Roman rule, some, like Juba, became auxiliary soldiers in the Roman army.

NUMIDIANS
Numidia was part of the Roman province of Africa. The name comes from the Latin for 'nomads' (people with no fixed home).

NO BARBARIAN REBELS MUST ESCAPE...

...ORDERS ARE ORDERS...

P-P-PLEASE SIR...

...OUR FATHER IS JUBA, A ROMAN CITIZEN.

WHO CARES!

YOU'LL JOIN THE OTHER PRISONERS!

OW!

WHILE OUR VILLAGE WAS BURNED TO THE GROUND...

...WE WERE TIED...

...AND LED AWAY.

SENATOR
A few hundred senators ruled Rome. These wealthy men were mostly from the nobility (upper classes).

EQUESTRIAN
Equestrians made up the second tier of Roman society. They were often army officers.

FREE BORN
Most of the Romans were ordinary citizens. They could be rich, poor or middle class.

FREED SLAVE
A slave who had been given his freedom became a citizen. Some freed slaves were rich.

SLAVES
Slaves were owned by Roman citizens or the Empire. They did all the hard work for no pay.

ROMAN SOCIETY

The people living in the Roman Empire were either citizens, foreigners or slaves. Citizens were of Roman descent. Some foreigners could become citizens after serving in the Roman army. Slaves were not citizens and had no rights at all.

PARTHIANS

The Parthians lived in what is now Iran. They fought many wars with the Romans but were never conquered by them.

EGYPTIANS

Egypt, the home of the greatest early civilisation, was a source of wonder to the Romans. The first emperor, Augustus, took over Egypt in 31 BCE.

ROMAN TRADE

Although the Roman Empire was conquered by soldiers, trade was important for holding it together. The Empire allowed merchants to buy and sell goods over a huge area. This helped make the inhabitants of the Roman world much better off than those living beyond its frontiers.

CLOTH
The Romans made cloth from wool and flax, but luxurious silk came overland all the way from China.

ANIMALS AND GRAIN
Thousands of exotic wild animals were imported from Africa. Grain came from many parts of the Empire.

HORSES AND OIL

Some of the best horses came from North Africa. Olive oil was produced in Italy but also imported from other areas.

WINE
By Juba's time, wine from southern Gaul was being exported all over the Roman world.

THE ROMAN WORLD

The Roman Empire included many nations and races who shared a way of life. The first Romans came from Rome and then from the region that is now Italy. In the later Empire, the Romans allowed a wide range of different peoples to call themselves Romans. They spoke the same language (Latin), obeyed the same laws and used the same money. They were all ruled by the Emperor, who was not necessarily of Italian birth.

...LYING DEAD ON A BATTLEFIELD.

...AND OF FATHER...

...AND MEMORIES OF HOME...

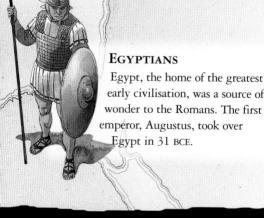

ALL I COULD THINK OF WAS FATHER.

WE WERE MARCHED TO THE PORT OF HIPPO...

AND LOADED ONTO A SHIP

...WITH OTHER PRISONERS OF WAR.

ALL WE HAD NOW

CONTINUED FROM PREVIOUS PAGE

TRAVELLING IN THE EMPIRE

In order to run their huge empire, the Romans needed to reach every part of it as fast as possible. Soldiers had to rush to wherever there was trouble. Merchants had to be able to move their goods from place to place. Governors and officials had to keep in touch with Rome. To do this, the Romans built a network of roads that crisscrossed the Empire. They made the roads as straight and smooth as possible so that travellers could move quickly.

MAKE WAY

The main purpose of roads was to move the Roman army around the Empire. Troops had priority, and other traffic had to give way to them. When in a hurry, soldiers walked about 50 kilometres (30 miles) in a day, although the normal rate was more like 30 kilometres (18 miles).

Roman soldiers marching

Two-wheeled chariot pulled by horses – used only by those of high rank

A pair of oxen joined by a wooden yoke

CARTING GOODS

Carts were the lorries of the Roman world. They were pulled by horses or oxen, although people sometimes had to help push the carts up steep hills or free the wheels if they got stuck in the mud. The most common loads were food and all kinds of textiles.

Dock-side crane powered by slaves walking inside giant treadmills

Swan figurehead

Wooden merchant sailing ship, steered by huge oars

WATER WAYS

The Mediterranean Sea was the Romans' biggest highway. It linked Italy to France, Spain, North Africa, Greece and Asia. Large merchant ships traded throughout the Empire. These ships mostly carried heavy goods, such as building stone, jars of wine or oil, bales of wool and even wild animals. Soldiers and slaves were often transported by sea, too.

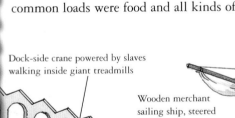

THE SHIP TOOK US TO ITALY...

...WHERE WE CONTINUED OUR WEARY JOURNEY.

THE NEW GUARDS WERE FAIR...

FOOD BREAK!

...BUT VERY STRICT.

DON'T EVEN THINK ABOUT ESCAPING!

OH, YEAH, TIN HEAD!

THAT WAS MAX, A BORN REBEL!

HE'S TROUBLE - I'LL HAVE TO WATCH HIM!

PSSSST!

PUBLIUS! WAKE UP!

OVER THE TOP

Whether using wood, stone or brick, the Romans were master bridge-builders. The foundations were laid in the summer, when the river was dry or small enough to be guided into another channel. Bridges were normally built to carry roads, but some carried water channels.

A long bridge, or viaduct, for carrying water

STORY CONTINUES ON NEXT PAGE

Paving stones

Ditch for collecting rainwater

Layers of stones and gravel

Foundation of local material, such as wood

CROSS-SECTION OF A ROMAN ROAD

BUILT TO LAST

Where possible, Roman roads were straight and wide. They were so well built that many have survived to the present day. First, a deep trench was dug and filled with a base material such as wood. Then came layers of small stones and gravel. Where paving stones were available, the surface was paved. The road surface was gently curved, forming a hump, to allow rainwater to run off into ditches at the sides.

Base of brushwood pounded into the ground

Checking the road is straight with a device called a *groma*

A road was laid in a trench over 1 metre (3½ feet) deep.

Wealthy citizen in a litter carried by four slaves

The broken wheel of this coach is being replaced.

PICKING UP LITTER

The wealthy were carried short distances in a litter – a chair with a roof above and curtains round it. Slaves balanced the carrying poles on their shoulders. Some important citizens travelled in large four-wheeled coaches. The technology of Roman vehicles was very advanced: some even had springs and a front axle that turned to make it easier to steer round tight corners.

I DREADED WHAT MIGHT HAPPEN WHEN WE REACHED THE IMPERIAL CAPITAL...

...ROME!

THERE WERE NO MORE ESCAPE ATTEMPTS.

THAT WAS NOTHING! NEXT SLAVE THAT MAKES A RUN FOR IT WILL DIE!

SLAVE?!!!!

...WHEN THEY BROUGHT MAX BACK.

DAD IS A METALWORKER.

YOU'VE PICKED THE LOCK?

I'LL DO YOURS, TOO.

NO! IT'S TOO RISKY!

MAX JUST LAUGHED AND SLIPPED AWAY.

WHY WOULDN'T YOU LET ME GO?

PUBLIUS FOUND OUT THE NEXT DAY...

A Life of Slavery

CONTINUED FROM PREVIOUS PAGE

Slaves were people who belonged to the state or one of its citizens and worked for them, usually without pay. In other words, they were a possession like a dog or a horse. Government slaves did most of the tough, back-breaking jobs, such as mining and road building. House slaves did household chores, such as washing or cooking. Slaves who could read and write had easier lives as teachers, secretaries and doctors. These valuable slaves were often Greek.

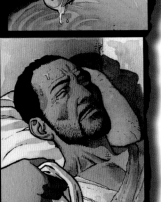

MEANWHILE...

THE GODS HAVE SPARED YOU, JUBA.

I MUST GET MY STRENGTH BACK!

Slave for Sale
Like Publius and Sabina, slaves were often prisoners who had been captured in war. They were then brought to Rome for sale. Slaves could be expensive, so buyers checked them over carefully to make sure there was nothing wrong with them.

Worked to Death
Rude or rebellious slaves might be sold to the mines. This was one of the worst jobs of all. Slaves had to work seven days a week to get precious metals or building stone from the ground. They were punished severely if they did anything wrong. Most mine slaves were literally worked to death.

Whip for disciplining slaves

Child Carers
Wealthy families employed female slaves as nannies. Those slaves whose own babies had recently died worked as wet-nurses. They breast-fed babies whose mothers had died or were unwilling to breast-feed their babies themselves.

Muscular Minders
An important Roman citizen rarely went out without a group of slaves. These slaves often included a secretary and some strong bodyguards. The bodyguards usually carried their owner's possessions and protected him or her from robbers or other dangers.

MY CHILDREN! I MUST FIND MY CHILDREN!

GOODBYE, JUBA! GOOD LUCK!

BACK IN ROME...

...PUBLIUS AND I WERE DISPLAYED AT A SLAVE MARKET.

YOU'VE GOT TWO FOR THE PRICE OF ONE!

THANK YOU, BRUTUS!

THEY SOLD US LIKE ANIMALS.

MY FATHER WAS A CITIZEN!

SHUT UP, SLAVE!

Crucifixion involved tying victims to a cross and leaving them to die.

A WARNING TO ALL

Slave revolts were very rare, partly because not all slaves were treated badly and partly because the punishments for rebellion were so cruel. The biggest revolt, in 73 BCE, was led the by the gladiator Spartacus. He and about 90,000 slaves managed to hold out for two years. After Spartacus's defeat by the Roman army, hundreds of his followers were executed by crucifixion.

WE THOUGHT OUR LUCK HAD CHANGED – AT LAST!

STATUS SYMBOLS

Owning lots of slaves was a way of showing off a person's wealth. Being waited on hand and foot made life pretty comfortable, too! In their wills, rich masters and mistresses often granted their slaves freedom. A freed slave might then become a Roman citizen. Those skilled slaves who were actually paid for their work could sometimes save up enough money to buy their freedom.

Wealthy people had many slaves.

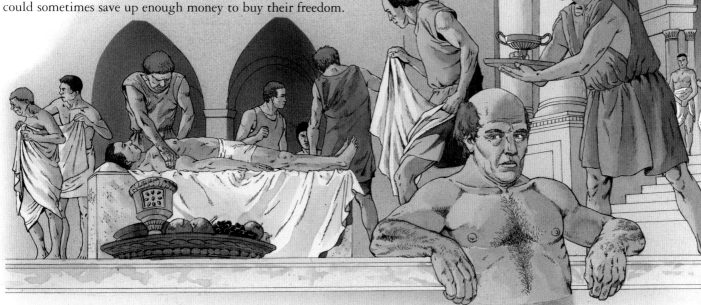

SHE SEEMS OK.

...DRUSILLA TOOK PITY ON US.

YOU MUST BE HUNGRY AFTER YOUR JOURNEY.

I'M DRUSILLA, THE HOUSEKEEPER HERE.

HAVING ONCE BEEN A SLAVE HERSELF...

DANCING GIRLS

No fancy Roman party was complete without music and dancing by highly trained slave girls. The dancers were usually not well treated. Life could be difficult for them as they grew older and their looks faded. Even so, they were better off than the slaves killed in gladiator shows to amuse the crowds.

VALUED SLAVES

Slaves who could read and write were prized, and their owners made sure they were well looked after. Some continued working for their owners even after they had obtained their freedom.

BUT HE WAS RARELY THERE.

WELCOME CHILDREN!

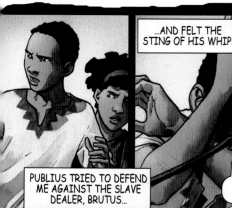

PUBLIUS TRIED TO DEFEND ME AGAINST THE SLAVE DEALER, BRUTUS...

...AND FELT THE STING OF HIS WHIP.

OW!

WE'D BETTER NOT MENTION FATHER AGAIN.

NO ONE BELIEVES US ANYWAY.

WE HAD BEEN BOUGHT BY A RICH NOBLE...

...WHO OWNED A VILLA OUTSIDE THE CITY.

15

WE WERE REALLY LONELY AT FIRST.

THEY WORKED US HARD...

...PUBLIUS AS A STABLE LAD...

STEADY, GIRL!

...AND ME AS A HOUSEMAID.

FETCH WATER FOR THE KITCHENS, SABINA!

2 STABLE MATES

In the stables a team of grooms and stable lads looked after the household's many horses. There was always a blacksmith, who made the horseshoes.

3 STORE ROOMS

The Romans did not have refrigeration so food had to be dried or smoked before it was stored. It was important to have the store rooms full before winter, when there was little fresh food available.

1 FARM WORK

As the last of the corn was harvested with scythes, an ox-drawn plough prepared the soil for next year's crop.

9 THE KITCHEN

The kitchen was like a restaurant kitchen, producing meals for dozens of people. Most cooking was done over an open fire, although bread and cakes were baked in circular ovens.

ROMAN VILLA

A villa was a large country house built around a courtyard. There were two basic types of villa: farm and luxury. Most, like the one here, were at the heart of a farming estate. Luxury villas were built by the very wealthy as places for relaxation. The emperors, for instance, had elegant seaside villas where they went in the summer to escape the heat. The finest villas had baths, gardens, drains, elegant decoration, running water and (in cold climates) underfloor heating.

BY DAY, WE WERE TOO BUSY TO THINK ABOUT HOME...

...AND WE SOON GOT USED TO THE ROUTINE.

HNNNNFFFF!

DRUSILLA WAS KIND, AND WE HAD ENOUGH TO EAT.

RACE YOU TO THE MILESTONE!

WE JUST HAD TO KEEP OUT OF THE WAY OF THE OWNER'S ROWDY SONS.

PUBLIUS AND I LOOKED AFTER EACH OTHER.

ARE YOU OK, PUBLIUS?

4 KITCHEN GARDEN
The villa's supply of fruit, vegetables, herbs and spices came from its own kitchen garden. Nearby beehives provided honey for sweetening food.

5 WATER SUPPLY
Water was brought to the biggest villas in special pipes and channels. This villa has a large pool. Slaves collected all the water needed for cooking, drinking and washing from here in buckets.

6 FORMAL GARDEN
The formal garden was laid out to a neat design. Along one side ran a shady walkway (colonnade) in which the family could take exercise without getting wet or sunburned.

7 THE ATRIUM
The heart of the villa was the atrium, which was a room for meeting guests and a living room. It was decorated with mosaics and often had a pool for collecting rainwater.

8 BEDROOM SPACE
A Roman bedroom was much emptier than a modern one. Clothes and bedding were stored in a wooden chest. Only the villa's owner and his family had the luxury of wooden beds.

I WON'T BE STAYING LONG...

...BUT I INTEND TO INSPECT THE RUNNING OF MY VILLA.

THERE ARE NEW SLAVES?

YES, MASTER. A BOY AND A GIRL.

WELCOME BACK, MASTER.

DRUSILLA!

A HORSEMAN...

...WHO IS IT?

BUT AT NIGHT...

...WE STILL MISSED FATHER TERRIBLY.

HAVE YOU SEEN ANY PRISONERS OF WAR FROM AFRICA?

NO, SORRY! TRY THE ROAD TO ROME.

YES, I'VE SEEN THEM...

...HEADING FOR ROME!

17

ROMAN CHILDHOOD

In Roman times, most boys went out to work at the age of 10 or younger. Girls also worked, usually doing jobs around the home, such as cooking, cleaning, baking and making clothes. Only rich families could afford to send their children to school. Boys were generally given more education than girls. They went to school from about age 7 to 16. Classes held around 12 pupils, and the teacher was often a Greek slave.

BULLAS

Nine days after they were born, Roman children were named in a ceremony. They were given a *bulla*, a charm that protected them from evil spirits. At 14 years old, boys threw away their *bullas* when they became adults. Girls gave up their *bullas* when they married.

TO BEAT OR NOT TO BEAT?

The Romans argued about whether beating children helped with their education. Thrashing slaves and animals was seen as normal. But many teachers argued that pupils should be encouraged with reason not threatened with the cane. Other teachers insisted that children would be spoilt if they weren't beaten regularly!

Greek schoolmaster – the Greeks were respected as the most learned people in the Empire.

Woman making cloth by weaving threads on a loom

Girl twisting wool into thread by hand

Younger boy writing with a pointed iron pen called a stylus on a wooden tablet coated with beeswax

LESSONS FOR GIRLS

Roman girls were not often educated after the age of 11. Before that, those whose parents could afford it received instruction in reading, writing and arithmetic. This was the same primary education as boys. A few young women were also taught Greek, the language of the highest learning. Girls were allowed to marry at 12, and very few were still single by the age of 20.

AGAIN, HADRIAN!

THE MASTER'S BOYS WERE AT THEIR LESSONS.

WHAT IS A NOBLE'S FINEST QUALITY?

DIGNITY, PROFESSOR - IT... ER... WINS RESPECT.

PRECISELY!

AND REMEMBER, DIGNITY IS HARD TO WIN...

...BUT EASILY LOST.

AHEM!

ALL RIGHT, TIME FOR DRINKS!

THANK YOU!

HADRIAN TREATED US WITH RESPECT...

...UNLIKE HIS BROTHER!

OOOOFF!

I	II	III	IV	V	VI	VII	VIII	IX	X	XX	XXX	XL	L	LX	LXX	LXXX	XC	C	D	M
1	2	3	4	5	6	7	8	9	10	20	30	40	50	60	70	80	90	100	500	1000

ROMAN NUMBERS

Romans wrote numbers by using a combination of seven letters: I, V, X, L, C, D and M. If a smaller number came before a larger number, the smaller number was subtracted from the larger number. For example, IX was 10 minus 1, which made 9. A smaller number after a larger one was added. So VIII was 5 plus 3, which made 8.

Boy practising oratory

LEARNING TO SPEAK

Speaking was just as important in Roman education as reading and writing. The art of public speaking – known as 'oratory' – came from the Greeks. It was particularly important for those planning careers in politics or the law, and there were professors of oratory in most major cities.

Papyrus was sold in rolls 10 metres (33 feet) long.

By Juba's time, the Roman alphabet had 23 letters. As it had no J, U or W, 'JUBA' was written 'IVBA'.

Older boy writing on sheets of papyrus, a form of paper made from reeds

The best pens had a bronze nib that was split to let the ink run down evenly.

A wax writing tablet

Vellum paper made from animal skins

Ink made from soot, gum and water

FUN AND GAMES

When they grew up, the male children of rich Romans were expected to serve in the army for a time. To prepare, they took plenty of exercise and played fighting games. Less violent amusement was had with toys, such as hoops, models, dolls, stilts, balls, kites and hobbyhorses. There were also board games similar to chess and backgammon.

Child plays with doll carved from wood.

Throwing dice – the Romans loved all forms of gambling.

Fighting game

Wooden hoop

...WE RAN AWAY...

...TO ROME!

QUIET, MY BEAUTY!

SO THAT NIGHT...

THE PUNISHMENT IS DEATH... BUT I CAN'T LEAVE PUBLIUS!

ARE YOU OK?

WHAT ARE YOU DOING, HADRIAN?

A NOBLE NEVER STOOPS FOR A MERE SLAVE!

THIS MAKES UP MY MIND...

...I'M GOING TO GET RID OF THAT SLAVE GIRL!

I TOLD PUBLIUS MY TERRIBLE NEWS.

YOU CAN'T GO, SABINA!

NO! WE'LL RUN AWAY!

I MUST!

CONTINUED FROM PREVIOUS PAGE

WE RODE ALL NIGHT.

THEN, JUST AS WE WERE NEARING ROME...

WHAT'S THAT AHEAD?!

WOAH!

LOOK OUT!

RUNAWAY HORSE!

1 MAKING BREAD

Bread was the basic food of most Romans. The dough was cooked in big round ovens.

2 WINERY

Watered-down wine, made from grape juice, was the Romans' favourite drink. The press in the middle of the room is for squashing juice out of grapes.

10 GRAFFITI

If the Romans found a blank wall, they scribbled on it! The city of Pompeii, for instance, had over 3,500 pieces of graffiti.

9 SHOP FRONTS

Shops were on the ground floor of houses or flats. Because they had no glass, they were more like market stalls. There was no refrigeration, either, so shoppers had to make sure the food was still fresh.

8 STONE HEROES

Statues decorated the main streets and meeting places. Some were religious. Others were of famous soldiers, politicians, speakers and writers.

PERHAPS WE CAN HELP!

QUICK, AFTER IT!

I THINK WE'RE GAINING!

GRAB THE REINS!

WOAH! STEADY! IT'S ALL RIGHT!!

WELL DONE, YOU TWO!

THIS NEW HORSE IS FAST BUT A BIT WILD!

WE'RE FROM THE BLUES CHARIOT-RACING TEAM.

WHERE ARE YOU HEADING?

LIVING IN ROME

3 BUILDING UP
A block of flats called an *insula* is under construction. Workers are covering the roof with clay tiles and plastering the walls. Most town-dwellers lived in flats like this one.

Rome was a thrilling city! With a population of around one million, it was by far the largest city in the Roman Empire. Some of it looked very grand, with elegant temples and beautiful statues. Its thousands of shops, market stalls and restaurants sold everything one could wish for, from hot food to the finest jewellery. But Rome was also dirty and overcrowded, with poor people living in tiny rooms. Traffic jams often blocked the streets, and thieves preyed on unwary citizens.

4 CLEAN CLOTHES
The people on the top floor of these flats are busy doing the laundry. Women are hanging the clothes out to dry in the sun. The woman in blue is weaving material on a loom.

5 BIG FANS
Cheered on by its supporters, a chariot-racing team parades through the streets. Roman race fans were as passionate about their team as football fans are today. Come on, you Reds!

7 PUBLIC WATER
Very few homes had their own running water. Public supplies were piped into the city's pools and fountains, from where people carried the water inside in buckets.

6 ANIMAL HOMES
Domestic animals, such as cows, pigs and chickens, were kept in city gardens – and even inside people's homes. Fortunately, most were better looked after than this unfortunate cow!

ESCAPED, EH?

YOU DON'T DENY IT? RIGHT, HERE'S WHAT I'M GOING TO DO...

HERE THEY ARE, BRUTUS!

MMMMMMPHHH!

BUT SUDDENLY...

ERR...GOING TO ROME...

...TO LOOK FOR WORK.

WORK? YOU'RE IN LUCK!

COME WITH ME - THE BLUES ALWAYS NEED GOOD STABLE HANDS.

AS WE ENTERED THE CITY...

...EVERYONE BEGAN CHEERING THE BLUES!

WAIT A MINUTE! I RECOGNISE THOSE TWO SLAVES!

COME ON, BOY!

WE FOLLOWED THE BLUES TO THEIR STABLES.

21

CONTINUED FROM PREVIOUS PAGE →

PLEASING THE GODS

At the time of Sabina and Publius, the Romans believed in many gods and spirits. To keep the gods happy, the Romans made them offerings, such as incense or food, and followed ceremonies. People also had to worship the Emperor. Refusing to do so was a serious crime – treason.

CERES VENUS MARS JUPITER JUNO APOLLO NEPTUNE

The Romans had hundreds of gods and goddesses. Jupiter was king of the gods. He was married to Juno, goddess of women. Ceres was the goddess of agriculture; Venus, the goddess of love; Mars, the god of war; Apollo, the god of the sun; and Neptune, the god of the sea.

Household shrine – the statues represented gods or the spirits of respected ancestors.

SPIRITS IN THE HOME

Each Roman household had its own spirits and gods. There were *lares*, who kept an eye on the whole house, and *penates*, who guarded the family's food. They were honoured at a household shrine, where the head of the house – usually the father – led regular worship. The family left an offering, such as bread or wine, or promised the god or goddess something in the hope that their wishes would be granted.

The flight of wild birds was thought to carry messages from the gods.

MAKING SACRIFICES

Animals were killed (sacrificed) to please the gods at an altar outside the temple. During a sacrifice, the words and movements had to be just right – even a dog barking might ruin the whole ceremony. The Romans believed that the greater the value of the animal, the more pleased the gods would be.

Priests were highly trained in making sacrifices. They also read signs from the gods, sometimes by examining the insides of the animals they had sacrificed.

Goat has been killed either to thank the gods or to beg a favour from them.

Animals had to be killed with one well-aimed blow of an axe.

Valuable, fat pig waiting to be sacrificed

Elderly woman soothsayer, believed to be able to see into the future

Left-side comic panels:

BRUTUS SOLD US TO A LAUNDRY OWNER.

I WASHED TOGAS, TREADING THEM ALL DAY.

PUBLIUS WORKED BLEACHING CLOTHES.

THE FUMES WERE POISONOUS...

... AND HE OFTEN PASSED OUT.

Bottom comic panels:

THE OVERSEER WAS MERCILESS.

OI! YOU SCUM!

GET UP AND GET BACK TO WORK!

BUT OUR NEW OWNER DIDN'T LIKE CRUELTY...

...AND OFTEN GOT ANGRY WITH THE OVERSEER.

WE SLEPT AT THE LAUNDRY.

IT WAS OUR ONLY CHANCE TO TALK.

THEN, ONE NIGHT...

IT'S THE OVERSEER!

CHRISTIANITY TAKES OVER

At first the Romans mostly ignored Christianity, a religion that began in and around Judea (modern-day Israel and Palestine) in about 30 CE. By Juba's time, some Christians were being persecuted because they refused to make offerings of incense to the Emperor's statue. But they continued to meet in secret, and their religion spread around the Roman world. Eventually, after 313 BCE, Christianity was adopted by the Emperor and became the major religion of the Empire.

New Christians were welcomed with a ceremony of washing known as baptism.

THE OVERSEER HAD GOT HIS REVENGE!

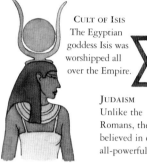

CULT OF ISIS
The Egyptian goddess Isis was worshipped all over the Empire.

JUDAISM
Unlike the Romans, the Jews believed in one all-powerful God.

MITHRAS
Mithras, the Persian sun god famous for killing a ferocious bull, was popular with Roman soldiers serving along the frontiers.

MIXED-UP GODS

As the Empire spread, non-Roman gods and goddesses were adopted by the Romans. The British goddess Sul, for example, was merged with the Roman Minerva, the goddess of arts and crafts. Similarly, the Greek Zeus, king of the gods, was combined with Jupiter.

BUT...WHAT FOR?

TREASON!

YOUR OVERSEER INFORMS US THAT YOU REFUSE TO PRAY TO THE EMPEROR.

VESTAL VIRGINS

The four or six Vestal Virgins were chosen from Rome's best families. They were not allowed to marry and had to serve for 30 years in the temple of Vesta, the goddess of the fireplace. Their most important job was keeping alight the sacred temple flame. The Romans believed that if the flame went out disaster would strike Rome.

The temple, built on sacred ground, housed statues of gods but was not a place of worship.

Architecture in Greek style, with massive columns, was the favourite temple design.

Emperors were worshipped as gods during their lifetime and after their death.

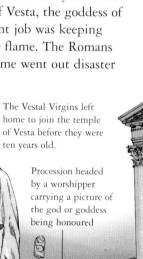

The Vestal Virgins left home to join the temple of Vesta before they were ten years old.

Procession headed by a worshipper carrying a picture of the god or goddess being honoured

BUT LATER, HE RETURNED WITH THE GUARDS.

YOU'RE UNDER ARREST!

OVERSEER, I TRUSTED YOU...

...LEAVE AND NEVER COME BACK!

HE'S A THIEF!

NEXT MORNING, THE OVERSEER BLAMED ME.

BUT IT WASN'T ME, MASTER!

NO! IT WAS HIM! HE'S THE THIEF!

LOOK!

23

CONTINUED FROM PREVIOUS PAGE →

MEANWHILE...

ROME AT LAST!

NOW TO THE SLAVE MARKETS.

I'M LOOKING FOR THE SLAVE DEALER, BRUTUS.

I'VE BEEN TOLD HE KNOWS WHERE MY CHILDREN ARE.

YOU'LL FIND HIM DOWN THE BATHS MOST MORNINGS.

BRUTUS, THE SLAVE DEALER?

RICH AND POOR

Ladies' jewellery

Life as a Roman very much depended on money and position in society. Rich nobles enjoyed all kinds of privileges, including top jobs and luxurious homes. The very poor had to scrape a living any way they could, often by begging or stealing. In between were the majority of Romans, who could be anything from wealthy merchants to shopkeepers or potters. But the Empire was a place of opportunity, where even freed slaves and foreigners could make their fortunes.

HOW DO I LOOK?

Rich Roman ladies usually wore make-up. They powdered their faces with chalk and lined their eyes with ash. Elaborate hairstyles and wigs were fashionable. Most Romans were naturally dark-haired so wigs made from the blond hair of prisoners of war were popular.

TOGA PARTY!

The Romans loved a good party. Those with money to spare held lavish banquets of rich food and spectacular amusements. Guests ate with their fingers or with spoons, and the meal could go on for several hours. Some parties were serious and intellectual, with poetry-reading and speeches. The more wild ones, where the red wine flowed freely, sometimes ended up as drunken riots.

Slave musicians play horns, pipes, a tambourine and a lyre.

Dancing slave girls

Guests reclined on couches and ate from low tables.

Slaves carry in a stuffed swan.

Poet entertains the guests.

Hosts showed off by providing lavish dishes and many courses.

WHO ARE YOU?

...AS SLAVES!

I AM JUBA, A ROMAN CITIZEN FROM MAURETANIA. I BELIEVE YOU SOLD MY CHILDREN...

I DON'T KNOW WHAT YOU'RE TALKING ABOUT.

NOW, GET LOST!

I WARN YOU, BRUTUS - I HAVE POWERFUL FRIENDS.

Shop selling wine

Carts could hardly get through the narrow streets.

People bought hot food from counters outside takeaways.

Children begging were a common sight.

IN THE BACK STREETS

The rubbish-strewn back streets of Rome crawled with dirt, disease and cruelty. Muggers lurked in dark corners. Beggars grabbed at passers by. Shopkeepers and street vendors cried their wares, while carts, donkeys, pedestrians and stray dogs jostled together in the crowded roadway. From time to time, plague swept through the city, killing thousands. Not surprisingly, few poor people lived beyond the age of 40.

WHAT ROMANS ATE

Bread was the basic food of most Romans. What went with it depended on wealth – the poor might be able to afford vegetables, eggs or a piece of sausage. The better-off also enjoyed a wide range of fruits, fish and meat. Most food was freshly prepared, making the Roman diet a healthy one. Only the rich had their own kitchens and ate at home. Ordinary Romans bought hot or cold snacks from takeaway shops or ate in cheap restaurants. The main meal was usually in the afternoon.

Wine mixed with water was the most common drink.

Bread was sometimes flavoured with cheese or honey.

Cheese was often made from goats' milk.

Fish and shellfish were popular with the well-off.

Poultry included chicken and duck.

Meat, such as pork, lamb and beef, was expensive.

...WHERE HE'S GOING!

HE WON'T NEED THEM...

WHAT ABOUT HIS DOCUMENTS?

PUT HIM IN THE CART!

BRUTUS HAS GOT PLANS FOR HIM!

LIKE WHO?

SENATOR HORTALUS!

I SEE... AND HAVE YOU SPOKEN TO HIM ABOUT THIS?

NOT YET, BUT I WILL...

...YOU'LL BE HEARING FROM ME!

HE'S GOT TO BE STOPPED!

THAT'S HIM!

CRACK!

25

CONTINUED FROM PREVIOUS PAGE →

WE WERE BROUGHT BEFORE A MAGISTRATE.

OUR OWNER, A CHRISTIAN, WAS SENTENCED TO DEATH FOR TREASON...

...AND WE SLAVES WERE SENT TO...

...THE COLOSSEUM...

...TO BE ARENA SLAVES – THE WORST JOB IN ROME!

CRIME AND PUNISHMENT

Roman law laid down strict rules that citizens had to obey. Public law was for punishing people who had harmed the state, such as traitors. Punishments were often harsh to discourage other wrong-doers. Private law dealt with quarrels between individuals, and cases were normally settled with fines. Some crimes were tried by a judge and a jury of up to 75 citizens. Other crimes were dealt with by officials called magistrates.

Under Roman law, parents were allowed to kill or abandon unwanted children. Others sometimes took these babies, often bringing them up as slaves.

OFF WITH HIS HEAD!

Death was the harshest punishment for an offence against Rome. The accused were often tortured first to make them admit their guilt. There were several gruesome ways of carrying out the death sentence, including burning, drowning in a sack and crucifixion (*see page 15*). Guilty soldiers were killed quickly by beheading because they had served the state. This was considered a merciful death. Nobles were usually allowed to commit suicide rather than face public execution, while the poor received the worst treatment of all.

Condemned soldiers were beheaded with a large sword.

AFTER THE KILLING...

...WE CLEANED UP.

GET A MOVE ON! THE PRISONERS ARE ON NEXT!

WE WERE NO BETTER THAN THE ARENA BEASTS...

...WAITING FOR DEATH.

SPEAKING UP

Public speaking (oratory) was vital in law making and in the law courts. No one was better at speaking in public than Marcus Tullius Cicero (106–43 BCE). He was a brilliant lawyer, who often successfully defended the accused in court with his arguments. Cicero also introduced ideas from ancient Greece into Rome, and his style of speaking influenced many later orators.

Statue of the famous orator Cicero

THROWN TO THE LIONS

One of the cruellest ways the Romans executed criminals was by unleashing wild animals on them at the public games. The animals were starved so they would be sure to pounce on their live meal and tear it apart. Such executions gave a terrifying warning to anyone thinking of committing a crime – and provided grisly entertainment at the same time. Christians who had committed the crime of treason by not worshipping the Emperor were sometimes killed in this way.

Execution beasts included lions, tigers, hyenas and panthers.

GO TO JAIL!

The lowest level of Rome's state prison was reached only through a narrow trapdoor. The dark, damp cell was used for holding enemies of Rome and for non-public executions. The word 'incarcerate', meaning 'imprison', comes from the name of Rome's prison, the Carcer.

Wooden carved eagle, the symbol of Rome

Continued from previous page

HOW CAN FATHER HAVE BEEN CONDEMNED TO DEATH?

WE MUST HELP H...

SSSHH! WE'VE GOT TO THINK - FAST!

WE NEED A DIVERSION!

I'LL SAVE HIM!

NO! I'VE GOT AN IDEA...

1 EXOTIC BEASTS

Animals slaughtered in the arena included elephants, lions, tigers, monkeys, bears, leopards, hippopotamuses, rhinoceroses, giraffes, camels, ostriches, wild boars, wolves and crocodiles.

2 BIG CROWDS

Spectators sat in rows in steep tiers. They were protected from the sun by a gigantic canvas awning. Suspended from 240 masts, it was operated by 1,000 sailors.

3 RISING PROPS

Scenery, like these palm trees, was raised up from below floor level on huge ramps operated by machinery.

12 WAY IN

There were 80 entrances: 76 for the general public, one for the city magistrates, one for the emperor and two for the performers.

11 FOUNDATION

As the Colosseum was built on marshy ground, about 250,000 cubic metres (327,000 cubic yards) of concrete had to be laid below ground level to make a solid foundation.

10 UNDERGROUND

The rooms under the arena floor were used for storing scenery, weapons, armour and even (temporarily) the dead bodies of humans and animals.

9 BRICK AND STONE

One million clay bricks and 100,000 cubic metres (131,000 cubic yards) of stone, cut into blocks and held together with iron clamps, were used to build the arena.

READY?...HEAVE!

COME ON!

IT'S MOVING!!

WE HAD OPENED THE LIONS' CAGE...

HIYAA!

HIYAA!

WHAT...?!!!

LOOK OUT!

AARGHHH!

THE COLOSSEUM

The Amphitheatrum Flavium, known today as the Colosseum, was the grandest amphitheatre in the Roman world. Begun by the Emperor Vespasian in 70 CE, it took more than ten years to build. Later emperors altered and improved it. The oval-shaped building seated around 50,000 spectators. Its floor rested on a network of underground rooms and passages that was linked to the arena by trapdoors.

4 EMPEROR'S BOX
The emperor, his family and guests had their own entrance to a private box beneath a colourful sun shade.

5 TOILET BREAK
With such big crowds, the building had to have lots of toilets! They were supplied with water from a system of lead pipes. Another system took away the waste.

6 BEAST V BEAST
Animals were made to fight each other – enraged bulls might fight elephants, for example. Gladiators also fought fierce animals.

8 FLOODING
As the underground rooms were not there when the Colosseum was first built, it is possible that the arena may have been filled with water. There would have been special games held on the artificial lake.

7 BIG GAME HUNT
Hunters all over the Empire worked to keep the Colosseum supplied with wild animals for its shows. Many thousands of creatures were captured and killed for the amusement of the Romans.

...TO FACE THE MOST POWERFUL MAN IN THE WORLD!

...AND TOOK US UP INTO THE ARENA...

THE GUARDS SEIZED US, TOO...

GET OFF!

RUN, CHILDREN, RUN!

PUBLIUS RUSHED IN TO TRY TO SAVE FATHER.

PUBLIUS?!!

OH MY SON! MY SON!

WE THOUGHT OUR PLAN HAD WORKED...

...BUT IT WAS TOO LATE...

...MORE GUARDS ARRIVED...

...THEY KILLED THE LIONS...

...AND GRABBED FATHER!

CONTINUED FROM PREVIOUS PAGE

SPECTATOR SPORTS

The Romans loved to watch sport, especially violent games. By the reign of Antoninus Pius, there were about 120 official games (*ludi*) a year – around one every three days. Games had once been religious festivals. By this time, they were just free entertainment put on by emperors to please the public. As each emperor tried to outdo his predecessor with more lavish entertainment, putting on games became a major Roman industry.

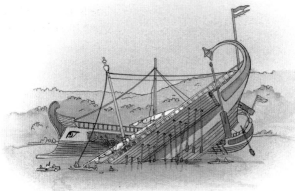

SEA FIGHT
Not many Romans got to see a real live naval battle so the games' organisers staged their own! They found a suitable lake or made one by flooding an arena. Then real ships and their crews fought sea battles in front of roaring crowds.

THRILLS AND SPILLS
Chariot racing was the oldest and most popular Roman entertainment. By Sabina and Publius's time, there were four teams: the Blues, Greens, Whites and Reds. Each was a professional team. Fights between their fans, who bet heavily on the races, were quite common. The light, two-wheeled chariots pulled by four horses raced at break-neck speed round seven circuits of the stadium. Successful charioteers became wealthy superstars, while the less skilled or unlucky were often killed.

There were three chariots for each team, making 12 in each race.

Teams were identified by colour: Blue, Green, White and Red.

WE THOUGHT WE WOULD DIE A HORRIBLE DEATH.

COURAGE, CHILDREN!

IS THIS PART OF THE GAMES, HORTALUS?

WHAT DO YOU MEAN, SIRE?

OUR FATE WAS IN THE EMPEROR'S HANDS!

PREPARE YOURSELVES FOR DEATH!

SIRE! I AM A ROMAN CITIZEN!

HOW DARE YOU!

BY THE GODS! IT'S... ...JUBA!

EXCUSE ME, SIRE, BUT HE'S TELLING THE TRUTH!

JUBA, MY FRIEND!

HORTALUS!

HOW DID THIS HAPPEN?

The Retarius gladiator carried a large net and a trident (a forked spear).

The Thracian gladiator fought with a short, curved sword.

A costumed figure with a hammer made sure the dead were really dead.

BLOOD AND SAND

Criminals, slaves, prisoners-of-war and even some women had to fight for their lives as gladiators. A few even volunteered! Gladiators were warriors trained for hand-to-hand combat in the sandy arena of an amphitheatre. There were rules about who could fight whom. Contests did not always end in death. A gladiator who had an opponent at his or her mercy might ask the crowd whether the defeated fighter should be killed or saved.

Slaves carried away the bodies.

CIRCUS MAXIMUS

Rome's largest chariot-racing stadium was the Circus Maximus, which held an amazing 200,000 people in three massive tiers of seats. The stadium was about 550 metres (1,800 feet) long and 137 metres (450 feet) wide. A full circuit, including tight turns round the posts at each end, was about 1,370 metres (4,500 feet). The centre of the Circus was decorated with statues put up by emperors and wealthy citizens.

Chariots often crashed and overturned.

THE END

...AT LAST!

...WE WERE TOGETHER AGAIN...

GO, BLUES!

...FATHER WAS MADE THE TEAM'S STABLE MANAGER...

WE GOT OUR JOBS BACK WITH THE BLUES...

IT WAS BRUTUS, THE SLAVE DEALER...

LATER...

...BRUTUS PAID FOR HIS CRIME...

...IN THE ARENA.

INDEX